STRAIGHT FROM THE HEART

A Devotional for Worship Leaders and Ministers

ELENORA MOUPHOUET

STRAIGHT FROM THE HEART. Copyright © 2024. Elenora Mouphouet. All Rights Reserved.

Printed in the United States of America.

No portion of this book may be reproduced, stored in a retrieval system, or transmitted in any form or by any means, except for brief quotations in printed reviews, without the prior written permission of DayeLight Publishers or Pastor Elenora Mouphouet.

ISBN: 978-1-958443-61-3 (paperback)

Scripture quotations marked (NIV) are taken from the Holy Bible, New International Version®, NIV®. Copyright © 1973, 1978, 1984 by Biblica, Inc.™ Used by permission of Zondervan. All rights reserved worldwide.

To:

_____

From:

_____

Date:

_____

Table of Contents

Acknowledgements 11
Preface 13
Introduction 15
Section One: Brokenness 17
    Brokenness in Worship: Giving Worship When the Heart Faints 18
    Seeking Answers in Distress: Offering Consistent Worship 19
    When it Seems Like the Enemy is Winning: All Odds Are Against You 20
    The Sweet Taste of Revenge: Tinted Worship 21
    Broken Spirit and a Contrite Heart: My Sins Are Before Me 22

Section Two: A Dark Place 25
    Bitterness: A Stumbling Block to Worship 26
    Overwhelmed: Yet I'll Worship 27
    Troubled: My Voice Still Resound His Worship 28
    Afraid I Am Losing Grip! Can I Still worship? 29
    Reproached Daily: Yet He Urges Me to Worship 30

Section Three: I Will Arise and Worship 33
    Morning and Evening: My Worship Will Ascend 34
    Oh, The Mercies of God: Every Day of My life 35
    He is Everything: The First and The Last 36
    Early Morning Proclamation: My Voice Shall He Hear in the Morning 37
    My Heart Is Fixed: Nothing Shall Make Me Falter 38

Section Four: Help Me Lord 41
    A Cry for Help: A Constant Need 42
    Lessons: He Teaches Me: He Reminds Me 43

Bold as a Lion: He Makes Me Fearless...44

Help From Zion: A Place of Refuge. 45

My Helper: He's Always with Me 46

Section Five: Sacrifice..**49**

Love Sacrifice: At All Times 50

Sacrifice of Thanksgiving: It Hurts But I'll Still Offer It.....................51

He Wants My Heart: Not My Garment..52

He Wants My Body: I Am His in Entirety..53

The Ultimate Sacrifice: Jesus Took my Place......................................54

Section Six: Love...**57**

Love is Obedience: Love is an Action Word 58

Love is Losing Sight of Oneself: Thinking of Another........................59

Wholehearted Love: Unconditional Love 60

Destructive Love: It Will Destroy You if You Let It 61

Your Love Is My Canopy: True Love Covers 62

Section Seven: Joy...**65**

Joyful Laughter: It Is Real...66

Fullness of Joy: It is Unstoppable 67

Joy of Salvation: I Found Joy When I Found Jesus 68

Tears: Sometimes a Good Thing..69

Joy Beyond the Trials: This Won't Last Forever 70

Section Eight: The Presence of God **73**

Lifeless Without You: I Come Alive in Your Presence 74

His Presence: God With Us..75

Entrance: Gladness is the Entrance Way..76

No Hiding Place: But I Desire to Hide Sometimes 77

Glory Belongs to God: Following His Ways Brings Him Glory 78

Section Nine: Chosen **81**

He Chose Me: Born For This Purpose 82

    No Other Opinion: Chosen to Bear Fruit 83

    Spoken For: I Am His 84

    Before My Parents: I Am His Treasured Possession 85

    Before the Earth's Foundation: He Was Intentional 86

Section Ten: Total Surender **89**

    Self-Denial: It's Not About Me 90

    We Are His Workmanship: He Makes Me Willing by His Spirit 91

    Doing His Will: Not Walking Without Direction 92

    Dangerous Game: Lose It for the Sake of Christ 93

    Surrendering is in Our Doing: Walking in His Ways 94

Section Eleven: Seek Him First **97**

    First Things First: We Must Keep This in Mind 98

    My Daily Bread: All Day, A Part of Me 99

    It's a Heart Thing: He Knows My Thoughts 100

    Seeking Him or Other Things: Is He First? 101

    My Heart's Desire: To Seek Him 102

Section 12: A New Song **105**

    A Song of Transformation: Telling My Life Story 106

    With My Soul: With My Spirit 107

    Sing of His Greatness: The World is Waiting 108

    He Has Done Marvelous Things: My Heart Sing 109

    Making Melodies: The Sound of Instruments 110

Conclusion **111**

About the Author **115**

This book is dedicated to every worship leader and minister who has sacrificed time, been through difficult times, and still had to lead God's people.

THANK YOU FOR YOUR SERVICE!

Acknowledgements

A book may be one of the hardest things to write, but the journey becomes easy and fulfilling as you proceed. I am grateful that God put some special people in my path to help make this book a reality. I am forever thankful for their love and sacrifice.

I'm grateful to Catherine Kennedy, Pastor Victorious Bongi, and Pastor Princess Otigbu, who read and edited this devotional. With all that the Lord has trusted me with, the time sacrificed and effort put into this devotional was worth it.

My twenty-five years spent working with worshippers inspired me to write this devotional. I will forever be indebted to Pastor David Owah Boakai for his invested time and teachings on how to plan and execute seminars and workshops.

A special thanks to Mrs. Augustina Sube, one of my beta readers; your time is highly appreciated.

Lastly, I appreciate my family, Apostle Edward Mouphouet and our little man, for their support and understanding while I penned my thoughts. I love you very much!

Preface

This devotional came from a place of love and encouragement for those standing on the front lines to advance the Kingdom of God. Worship leaders experience many things that congregation members go through, but the expectations are different. Sometimes, we serve wounded, hurt, and discouraged. We serve from a place of sacrifice while the entire world expects us to be superheroes.

This devotional is an insight into some of the countless things. As a worship leader, as you use this devotion, you will begin to have encounters that will elevate your ministrations to God and His people. As sin increases in the world, let this devotion help lead you back to the place of sweet surrender. My heartfelt prayer is that as you journey through this devotional, the Spirit of God will touch your heart in every way possible in the mighty name of Jesus Christ, our Lord and savior.

Introduction

Congratulations! You made a wise choice by purchasing this devotional. I invite you to take this journey with me through these pages written in nine sections; your outlook on ministry will change.

I have taught and led worship for over twenty-four years in different countries through our worship ministry called Judah's Generation and Worship Services. We have impacted the lives of many worshippers during our seminars, conferences, and worship retreats. It is out of these experiences that I bring you **Straight from the Heart: A Devotional for Worship Leaders and Ministers**. It touches on what most people ignore or misunderstand about worship.

Worship leaders are always on the front line, leading worship and ensuring that all goes well with the congregation and music teams while expected to minister with excellence at the same time. We make sacrifices by spending countless hours in preparation, but sometimes, the one ministering goes unnoticed. The body of Christ falls short in making an impact by ensuring that those who lead the congregation are spiritually healthy.

Like everyone else, worshipers sometimes need a shoulder to cry on because they face real-life situations like heartaches, and they too need spiritual strengthening. Worshippers are human beings and can get depressed at times and are hurt and misunderstood.

This devotional is birthed out of a biblical approach and experiences to find answers in your brokenness. It will help you heal, redirect your thoughts, revive you, and set you on the path of fulfilling your purpose as a worshiper. The information in this devotional will help you face the challenges of being a leader in the worship arts ministry and help you guard your heart to lead worship from a place of love.

Section One

Brokenness

Brokenness in Worship:

Giving Worship When the Heart Faints

"But as for me, afflicted and in pain— may your salvation, God, protect me. I will praise God's name in song and glorify Him with thanksgiving. This will please the LORD more than an ox, more than a bull with its horn and hooves." (Psalm 69:29-31 – NIV).

One of the most challenging times to offer true worship is when a man's spirit is crushed, yet it is precisely in these moments that the grace of God can shine brightest, transforming despair into hope and weakness into strength.

Affliction, hurt, bitterness, pain, and sorrow can rob you of the desire to offer true worship. We must see affliction as an opportune time to worship, for when the heart faints, God is there to carry and uphold you. He will put a new song of thanksgiving in your mouth and turn your sorrow into dancing. The sacrifice of time, weeping, sleepless nights, and dedication cannot be compared to the times He will carry and comfort you in His presence.

It is the will of God for His children to give Him thanks in all things, in good times and unfavorable times. We often show gratitude when all is well but shy away in trying times. Let us always practice thankfulness, even when our hearts have been broken. So, always glorify Him!

Seeking Answers in Distress:

Offering Consistent Worship

"Do not let the floodwaters engulf me, or the depths swallow me up, or the pit close its mouth over me. Answer me, LORD, out of the goodness of your love; in your great mercy, turn to me." (Psalm 69: 15-16 – NIV)

When the temporary waves and troubles of life take the place of your joy and peace, it may seem like God is so far away. At times, it feels like your prayers are hitting the ceiling and bouncing back in your face. Your heart yearns to hold on, and your flesh is crushed under what may appear like an inferno of mishaps. Encourage yourself. Let your praise and worship rise from that inferno and offer heartfelt worship to God, our Father, and by doing so, you are offering a sacrifice of praise. He is right there—closer than you think—to carry you at that moment.

We seek answers out of anxiety, make decisions out of fear, and neglect the source of our strength, and at that moment, we are like the Psalmist beckoning God to come closer when He has always been there. In distress, He is always there. It may feel like He is not there with you, but God has the integrity to keep His Word.

When it Seems Like the Enemy is Winning:

All Odds Are Against You

"You know how I am scorned, disgraced and ashamed; all my enemies are before you. Scorn has broken my heart and has left me helpless; I looked for sympathy, but there was none, for comforters but I found none. They put gall in my food and gave me vinegar for my thirst." (Psalm 69:19-21 – NIV).

Sometimes it seems like your enemies have the upper hand, and you are losing everything the Lord has given you. You may be in a time of pain, and your heart is torn apart with hurts and pains unexplainable. Challenges in life may seem to cover your very existence, leaving you to believe that you cannot recover, but it is in these darkest hours that the unwavering light of God's presence promises renewal and a path to redemption. Your cry for help seems to go unheard, and comfort cannot be found. Overwhelmingly, your heart is overtaken with bitterness.

Looking for help, comfort, and peace in every place may not be the best solution for your troubles, so hold on and pour out your heart in His presence. Take comfort in this and know that the Holy Spirit (The Comforter) is with you. When we step into the place of worship in a challenging situation, our problems will become insignificant to our eyes.

The Sweet Taste of Revenge:

Tinted Worship

"Do not take revenge, my dear friends, but leave room for God's wrath, for it is written: "It is mine to avenge; I will repay," says the Lord. On the contrary: "If your enemy is hungry, feed him; if he is thirsty, give him something to drink. In doing this, you will heap burning coals on his head. Do not be overcome by evil but overcome evil with good." (Romans 12:19-21 - NIV).

The sweet taste of vengeance is one of the weapons in the world's arsenal. The system of the world tells us the best way to satisfy a score and appease one's anger, frustration, or hurt is to repay evil for evil—revenge oneself. Revenge is like a double-edged sword, covered with temporary satisfaction and more pain. We take the place of God when we avenge ourselves.

The evil desire for revenge will cloud the heart with bitterness and water down our worship. Leave room for God's wrath. Be good to those who hurt you, and your worship will be pure. Avenging oneself is equivalent to an attempt to become the ultimate authority in your case, forgetting that true justice and vindication lie in the hands of God. While you wait for God's justice, keep your heart pure and worship like it never happened.

Broken Spirit and a Contrite Heart:

My Sins Are Before Me

"My sacrifice, O God, is a broken spirit; a broken and contrite heart you, God, will not despise." (Psalm 51:17 – NIV).

When your heart is broken, nothing comes so easily than the thought of "payback." Your mind is captivated by thoughts of making your offender experience the same pain he or she has caused you, but then you hear the gentle, small voice of the Holy Spirit telling you that your thoughts are impure and ungodly. Suddenly, your thoughts are before you like a mirror, and you can see your sins clearly.

Sometimes it takes the visibility of our sinful thoughts to reveal how far we are from God. Thinking about hurting someone lands you in the same category as the person who hurt you. Our hearts should be broken, and we should humble ourselves, repent, and forgive. You have a choice today. What will you do? Abba Father will always accept a person who turns away from their wicked ways for the sake of Christ. It will be difficult to enter the presence of God and be used in a greater way by God if we do not learn the simple principle of having a clean heart before God. A broken heart before God is priceless.

MY REFLECTIONS

MY DECISIONS

"I will instruct you and teach you in the way you should go, I will counsel you with my loving eye on you." (Psalm 32:8 – NIV).

Section Two

A Dark Place

Bitterness:

A Stumbling Block to Worship

"Get rid of all bitterness, rage and anger, brawling and slander, along with every form of malice." (Ephesians 4:31 – NIV).

See to it that no one falls short of the grace of God and that no bitter root grows up to cause trouble and defile many." (Hebrews 12:15 – NIV).

Bitterness is the after-effect of hurt. It leaves you angry and self-conceited and can damage your spirit, if you let it. Your life can take a drastic turn, headed in the path of destruction, if you continue to be bitter. For your sake and to keep a healthy spirit for worship, let it go.

I understand that healing from hurt is a process, but you need first to have the desire to let it go; consciously decide to let it go, and desire to be healed. It may be challenging, but the Holy Spirit is always present to help you through the process, comfort you, and heal you of the most profound hurt. Do not look on the one who has hurt you, but instead look upon the one who can heal you. Let nothing contaminate your worship. Always give a "heartfelt worship!"

Overwhelmed:

Yet I'll Worship

"So my spirit grows faint within me; my heart within me is dismayed. I remember the days of long ago; I meditate on all your works and consider what your hands have done. I spread out my hands to you; I thirst for you like a parched land." (Psalm 143:4-6 – NIV).

Challenging situations can weigh on your spirit with unexpected, overwhelming power. If you are not careful as a worshipper, there is a tendency to forget the goodness of the Lord and how He suffered for you. During these dark moments, look back and draw strength from how He saved you. Consider His miracles, signs, and wonders.

Remember that God is faithful, and He is the Alpha and Omega, so He knows the ending of your struggle. Be like the Psalmist who, feeling overwhelmed in his darkest hour, lifted his hands towards our Father. If you can refocus your attention on the goodness of God, you will find that He has a plan to bring you out. Ironically, challenging times can bring out the best in us, which can be greater than the pain itself if we don't let it destroy us. Please let it go!

Troubled:

My Voice Still Resound His Worship

"I am bowed down and brought very low; all day long I go about mourning. (Psalm 38:6 - NIV).

You kept my eyes from closing; I was too troubled to speak. (Psalm 77:4 - NIV).

For the director of music. Of the Sons of Korah. According to alamoth. A song. God is our refuge and strength, an ever-present help in trouble. (Psalm 46:1 – NIV).

When trouble comes, it can leave you speechless and sleepless—mourning becomes your routine—but God can bring you out. No matter what, God, our Father, by His precious Holy Spirit, will help you overcome when you are bowed down in worship to Him. He will lift your head in due season.

We must learn to draw strength from the Lord, knowing He is our covering and shelter. God is more significant than your troubles; He is fully aware of all our problems and those to come. He is not ignorant of what you are going through, and we must trust that He has a plan. Our worship cannot be impactful without trust in God. Troubles fuel your worship with the knowledge that God is faithful in keeping His promises and can shift the atmosphere around you and give you peace. So let your praise come from the deepest part of you, for God is great, and He will see you through.

Afraid I Am Losing Grip!

Can I Still worship?

"The waves of death swirled about me; the torrents of destruction overwhelmed me." (2 Samuel 22:5- NIV).

"When I am afraid, I put my trust in you." (Psalm 56:3 – NIV).

Fear not rebuked and brought under control can become a mighty force that cripples you emotionally and distorts your outlook on life. It can paralyze and hinder you from moving forward, so do not allow fear to rule and dictate how you fulfill your purpose. When you are afraid, know that God is right there with you. He can carry you in His arms and give you peace that the human mind cannot comprehend. Keep your eyes on Him because He can help you conquer your fears.

Fear is the opposite of faith; you cannot stand on biblical principles and act on them when you are under the power of fear. Don't lose hope; let faith arise, and trust God with your heart. Remember, He is the Maker and Creator of your being; He knows your name and has an excellent plan for you. Don't forget to worship the One (your Abba Father) who conquers the greatest fear. Let worship arise because if He conquered death, He will bring you out.

Reproached Daily:

Yet He Urges Me to Worship

My bones suffer mortal agony as my foes taunt me, saying to me all day long, "Where is your God? (Psalm 42:10 - NIV).

"Remove from me their scorn and contempt, for I keep your statutes." (Psalm 119:22 – NIV).

Have you ever felt like your prayers are not being answered? Have you prayed for the thing that matters the most to you, and it seems like the heavens froze over you? Everything else works perfectly fine, but you feel invisible and hidden from the sight of God. It seems like you have done everything out of love for the Lord—tried to live a holy life, kept His Word—however, it has become apparent that when people do not see visible traits of change in your circumstances, they begin to tag you, call you names, and even despise you. Sometimes even the ones you love question where the God you serve is. I encourage you to fasten your seatbelt a little tighter. God still has a plan, so let your worship flow from a heart of expectancy.

MY REFLECTIONS

MY DECISIONS

"I will instruct you and teach you in the way you should go, I will counsel you with my loving eye on you." (Psalm 32:8 – NIV).

Section Three

I Will Arise and Worship

Morning and Evening:

My Worship Will Ascend

"A psalm. A song. For the Sabbath day. It is good to praise the LORD and make music to your name, O Most High, proclaiming your love in the morning and your faithfulness at night." (Psalm 92:1-2 – NIV).

In moments of overwhelm, when your strength wanes, embracing coming before Your Father with your worship—gratitude, adoration, and thanksgiving—ushers in unparalleled joy and gladness. This act of devotion, reflecting on the steadfast faithfulness of God, becomes a wellspring of renewal.

God's love, boundless and unfailing, transcends our weariness and physical limitations. By meditating on His goodness, we allow His love to flourish within us, nurturing a spirit of gratitude for every blessing, no matter how small. It is with such a heart, overflowing with thankfulness, that our praise becomes most sincere and profound.

Every worshiper must be able to see the handiwork of God through the things we consider minor. Gratitude will build our faith and enhance our worship. However, if we are ungrateful, we can never be able to ascend to the very presence of God. Worship should be a constant thing on our lips, regardless of the time of the day or the way we feel or think.

Oh, The Mercies of God:

Every Day of My life

"The LORD'S lovingkindnesses indeed never cease, For His compassions never fail. They are new every morning: great is thy faithfulness. They are new every morning; Great is Your faithfulness." (Lamentations 3:22-23 – NIV).

As we walk with the Lord, His ways amaze us, and sometimes, we can't help but say, *"Oh, wretched one like me. What have I done to obtain the mercy of God? I am unworthy to receive such."*

Indeed, it is unmerited favor, for it is by the mercies of God that His wrath has not come upon us. We abuse and take advantage of the grace of God; we disregard God's mercy and use it as a free getaway card to live like unbelievers, yet He never stops loving us.

If you cannot find a reason to praise and worship God, let this be an encouragement to you today. The many times we sin and abuse the grace of God and our actions warrant judgment, He wraps us in His arms and lovingly shows us the right way back. So, instead of running away from Him, keep in mind that when the day breaks, His mercy is already renewed.

He is Everything:

The First and The Last

"In the morning, LORD, you hear my voice; in the morning I lay my requests before you and wait expectantly." (Psalm 5:3 – NIV).

It is easy to lay in bed, drowning in the cares of this world instead of casting our cares on Jesus, the author and finisher of our faith. He desires to hear your voice, even in the darkest moments of your life. He desires to fellowship with us, and there is no better time to have that alone time with the Lord.

When everybody is sleeping and the world seems to stand still, it is a time that should be cherished and kept sacred. Sometimes our schedules and daily routines hinder us from spending time with the Lord, as seen in the captioned scripture, but if we plan our days, months, and year with God in mind, our body, soul, and spirit will adjust.

We must realize and adopt the mindset that God is not an option; He is the only option, and our activities should be planned around Him. Begin today and schedule your day with the Father in mind. Begin your day with Him and end your day with Him in worship.

Early Morning Proclamation:

My Voice Shall He Hear in the Morning

"But I will sing of your strength, in the morning I will sing of your love; for you are my fortress, my refuge in times of trouble." (Psalm 59:16 – NIV).

Declare this over your life: "For the nights You carried me and the days You protected me, I will lift my voice and declare Your greatness in the land of the living. My voice will be heard early in the morning like a trumpeter and watchman, screaming from the top of my voice and making melodies in my heart, singing a new song to You. You wake me up in the morning and keep me in my right mind."

Why should I be silent when I have the most powerful and merciful God as my Father and defense? Early will He hear my voice in the morning.

When a worshiper gains understanding and wisdom of God's unfailing love, it is easy to worship beyond your feelings. He is not only a God of love but fights for us when and where we cannot resist. He becomes our safe place in times of trouble and storms; as you worship, ponder these things.

My Heart Is Fixed:

Nothing Shall Make Me Falter

"My heart, O God, is steadfast, my heart is steadfast; I will sing and make music." (Psalm 57:7 – NIV).

Nothing is more peaceful than having a mind and heart fixed on God. Nothing can be compared to understanding how to fix our eyes on Jesus as we walk according to His Word. When your heart is set on anything in life, it gives you the strength and courage to pursue it. In the same way, once a man's heart is fixed on God, he brings Him pleasure.

Having a heart fixed on the Lord allows us to have encounters with the Holy Spirit and enables us to become more knowledgeable and gain wisdom. When your heart is fixed on God, everything else becomes secondary; your decisions are aligned with the Word of God, and He becomes the object of your worship. With a fixed heart on God, you will desire to please Him and grow your relationship with Him. Worship becomes so effective when we fix our eyes on Jesus. When we are not focused on Christ, we lose our sense of direction, and instability will hinder our worship.

MY REFLECTIONS

MY DECISIONS

"I will instruct you and teach you in the way you should go, I will counsel you with my loving eye on you." (Psalm 32:8 – NIV).

Section Four

Help Me Lord

A Cry for Help:

A Constant Need

"Hear, LORD, and be merciful to me; LORD, be my help." (Psalm 30:10 – NIV).

One of the most encouraging things about our Father is that you can call on Him and talk to Him about anything. When you are at your wit's end, be sure to cry out for help and petition the One who is not deaf or silent to the cry of the righteous; He is faithful in keeping His promises. He will show you mercy.

Regardless of what you may have done or what sin you have committed, all you need to do is come before His throne and cry for help. He has provided the Holy Spirit to help us overcome. When life throws us an unexpected blow, we can rest assured that we will come out victorious. He wants us to call on Him in times of need. Sometimes, it is difficult to ask for help when we are adults. It is difficult to ask someone to do anything for us, but our Father wants us to ask Him for help. Everyone needs help at some point in their lives, and as worshippers, we must understand that it is normal to ask for help so we can be healed, get direction, or get wisdom so our worship will not be hindered.

Be encouraged to worship!

Lessons:

He Teaches Me; He Reminds Me

"But the Advocate, the Holy Spirit, whom the Father will send in my name, will teach you all things and will remind you of everything I have said to you." (John 14:26 – NIV).

Walking with the Lord and being led by the Holy Spirit is comforting. Today, as I meditate on this scripture, I can't help but ask the Spirit of God to teach me all I need to know about true worship until it becomes my lifestyle.

Without knowledge, we perish, and as worshippers, we must be knowledgeable. You can only lead when you have had some experience, or it would be a case of the blind leading the blind. When it is time to lead worship, the Spirit of God will remind you what you have learned as you lead the people in the presence of the Lord. Always strive to be in a place to heed His promptings when He reminds you of the goodness of God. Remember to be thankful constantly!

Bold as a Lion:

He Makes Me Fearless

So we say with confidence, "The Lord is my helper; I will not be afraid. What can mere mortals do to me?" (Hebrews 13:6 – NIV).

Declare this over your life, "I will not fear because the Lord is my helper. I will boast in the Lord; without Him, I am nothing but a weakling. The Lord is the Almighty, the most powerful God, and holds all power in His hand. He overcame fear and death on the cross of Calvary. Therefore, I can boldly say He is for me, and no one can stand against me. I am not afraid, and neither am I intimidated."

Take courage because He is with you, and He is the Creator of all, including the one imposing fear on you. Fear is a force that cripple your ability to worship freely. You must get rid of all fears before you stand to lead God's people into His presence. Regardless of what you are afraid of, know that God is your Helper, and He will be with you in all circumstances.

The Holy Spirit is your Helper. Rejoice!

Help From Zion:

A Place of Refuge

"May he send you help from the sanctuary and grant you support from Zion." (Psalm 20:2 – NIV).

The Lord can connect you with people in the Kingdom of God who will help you. Some God-fearing Christians can help you in a humble way without being judgmental. The Lord can seek out help from His house.

When you feel like you are all alone, remember there are still good people God can use to bless you. When you need assistance, God can connect you with a sister or brother in Christ. He can give you spiritual parents. He can give you spiritual children. These people will support you in prayer through a transitional period. You must keep holding on faithfully and believe that God can do this. I know that sometimes you can't trust just anyone in the church, but there are still some people you can trust. Don't hesitate to ask for help from Zion.

As a worshipper, you cannot be isolated; you cannot be alone. Hold tight to His hands, for help is coming!

My Helper:

He's Always with Me

"Be strong and courageous. Do not be afraid or terrified because of them, for the LORD your God goes with you; he will never leave you nor forsake you." (Deuteronomy 31:6 – NIV).

When we are hurting or disappointed, sometimes we seek help from things or people we trust; other times, we withdraw and bury our feelings in our work and the songs we compose. We forget that either option may not be the best if we are not seeking help from God through His Holy Spirit who is our Helper. We seek help in things like food, shopping, money, and humanity. While we are looking for comfort in the wrong places, the Holy Spirit is right where we are. He is forever willing to help us in these seasons of our lives; He is there to walk us through the process of healing. He is there to restore us and our trust in humanity.

In these seasons as believers, we must turn to God for help. He is well able to provide in all capacities. Total reliance on God is the key to receiving genuine help. He can direct you to who to speak to and share your feelings with. There are still people who are like a "pillow to cry on" during these times. Let God direct you, and let His Holy Spirit help you.

MY REFLECTIONS

MY DECISIONS

"I will instruct you and teach you in the way you should go, I will counsel you with my loving eye on you." (Psalm 32:8 – NIV).

Section Five

Sacrifice

Love Sacrifice:

At All Times

"The reason my Father loves me is that I lay down my life—only to take it up again." (John 10:17 –NIV).

Sacrifice is a high price to pay for anything in life. You must deny yourself, and, at times, you must let go of the things and people dear to you. Many times, we escape this part of our walk with the Lord. Sometimes, we must make sacrifices to please the Lord. If giving up that friendship or traveling away from family for a long time is difficult, then you may not be ready for service in the Lord's vineyard.

When you are in love, you sacrifice—you give up your rights and privileges; the Lord delights in our sacrifices. These are the times that His love is even more evident than other times. We must learn to offer the sacrifice of praise, making our praise and worship costly. During those times, let your heart sing with love.

Sacrifice is an expression of love. We are saying to our Father, "I can give up anything for You in sacrifice." Don't despise the time of sacrifice, but ask the Lord to teach you the true meaning of sacrifice and lay down your life like Jesus, our Savior, did.

Sacrifice of Thanksgiving:

It Hurts But I'll Still Offer It

"Sacrifice thank offerings to God, fulfill your vows to the Most High. Those who sacrifice thank offerings honor me, and to the blameless I will show my salvation." (Psalm 50:14,23 – NIV).

When speaking of thanksgiving, you must be a person of gratitude to be thankful. We can develop a heart of gratitude by being grateful for the things we see God do in our lives daily. Sometimes we may not have all we want, but the Bible tells us that we should give thanks in all things, in all circumstances or situations.

We all desire pleasure and comfort; sometimes, we may not have it that way. Sacrifice means putting the needs of others before our needs and stepping out of our comfort zone to help. The sacrifice of thanksgiving is giving thanks sacrificially, even when we don't want to or feel like it. As worshipers, it is a requirement and not a choice. Offering sacrifice of praise is when we don't want to, but faith tells us to; that is why it is a sacrifice. So, when you don't want to give thanks in terrible situations, remember that your thanksgiving in that moment is your sacrifice.

He Wants My Heart:

Not My Garment

"My sacrifice, O God, is a broken spirit; a broken and contrite heart you, God, will not despise." (Psalm 51:17 – NIV).

We must realize that God is not carried away or takes pleasure in works—the fans and conferences—but He is more concerned about our hearts and motives. When we worship, we strive to lead from a place of humility. Worship is a place of sacrifice; we can lay our lives before His throne in humility and surrender all to Him. This is the sacrifice that is acceptable to Him.

We can be used for His glory if we come in brokenness and humility. When I think of His love for humanity and how He paid the price on the cross for our sins, I realize that no matter how much we have or accomplish, we can never repay Him for dying in our place, but we can dedicate our lives to work for and worship Him in spirit and truth. Jesus is a perfect expression of sacrifice. He left His home in glory and became like a sinner to save mankind. Let's remember that when we worship!

He Wants My Body:

I Am His in Entirety

"Therefore, I urge you, brothers and sisters, in view of God's mercy, to offer your bodies as a living sacrifice, holy and pleasing to God—this is your true and proper worship." (Romans 12:1 – NIV).

We are concerned about every detail of every minute of our lives; how we live, and what we do every second of the minute. We hear about others and their situations, but we are so consumed with ourselves that we forget others. Our actions show our heart condition and the state of our mind. On the contrary, God is concerned about our hearts and bodies and wants us to have a humble heart and be broken in His presence when we worship Him.

Give God thanks for showing us that He cares about the condition of our hearts. To live fully, we must be willing to learn to align our body, mind, and spirit with the teachings of God's Word. If you have not understood or sacrificed for the Kingdom of God, seek wisdom from God because He takes pleasure in our body being a living sacrifice for good works. We must be a sacrifice that is holy, devoted, consecrated, and always pleasing in the sight of God. We belong to Him!

The Ultimate Sacrifice:

Jesus Took my Place

"He is the atoning sacrifice for our sins, and not only for ours but also for the sins of the whole world." (1 John 2:2 – NIV).

Jesus Christ became the ultimate sacrifice for humanity. When you get a revelation about Jesus Christ's death on the cross, you understand fully that Jesus paid a high price for you and me. The best way we can appreciate Him for all that He has done is to lavish Him with praise and worship. Think about the sacrifice you are making today, including the sacrifices you will make in the future, then compare it to what Jesus did on the cross. You will soon find out that His sacrifice outweighs yours.

When we go through difficult times, genuine praise and worship are far from our lips, but everyone must give the "Sacrifice of Praise." We have been called to offer ceaseless praise. Though the times and seasons may change, Abba Father deserves our worship from the valley to the mountain top. We praise Him in the valleys because He is there with us; He is the same God in different seasons of our lives. He never changes, and He never leaves us!

MY REFLECTIONS

MY DECISIONS

"I will instruct you and teach you in the way you should go, I will counsel you with my loving eye on you." (Psalm 32:8 – NIV).

Section Six

Love

Love is Obedience:

Love is an Action Word

"If you love me, keep my commands." (John 14:15 – NIV).

Love is the most powerful tool in the world today. Love can make you subscribe to anything and cause you to change who you are. There are different kinds of love, but only the "Agape" love lasts forever. This is the kind of love that pushes us to obey God. When we follow the commandments of the Lord and walk in His ways, we express our love for Him. Obedience is essential as we walk with the Lord.

Every believer must learn to hear and obey the Word of God at all costs. When He speaks, we do as He has spoken. When we read the Bible, we should practice what we have read in the Holy Scriptures. When we worship, we worship based on Scripture; we cannot afford to worship based on how we feel we should worship God. Our Father has set up principles by which we should worship Him. We must lead and glorify our Father, Elohim, in the way He has written in His Word. Let's follow His principles and be an example. Show your love by obeying!

Love is Losing Sight of Oneself:

Thinking of Another

"and walk in the way of love, just as Christ loved us and gave himself up for us as a fragrant offering and sacrifice to God." (Ephesians 5:2 - NIV).

We cannot say we love God and hate our brother, sister, or neighbor. Love makes you value someone else more than yourself. Our love for God should be expressed in our attitude towards our neighbors, exhibiting our love for one another, and putting our goals, desires, and dreams second to follow Christ; that is true love.

Love seeks the progress and advancement of others; it will push us to do everything possible to see our neighbor prosper. When we profess that we love God, our actions should not contradict what we profess. Loving God and loving our neighbor must be done genuinely. The expression of love for our neighbors is a direct revelation of how much we love God. Love cannot be tinted or faked; it can never be copied or pretentious and, as worshipers, the love of God must always exude from us so that it can translate in our rendition and through our instruments playing. Love unconditionally!

Wholehearted Love:

Unconditional Love

"Love the LORD your God with all your heart and with all your soul and with all your strength." (Deuteronomy 6:5 – NIV).

Love is expressive. When we love genuinely, it shows in our actions, meaning our efforts exhibit the measure of love in our hearts. Intense love—deep love—requires body, soul, and spirit. We cannot say we love God, and there is no action to demonstrate what we feel in our hearts. True love provokes actions; true love will shape your life because someone in love does everything to please the one they love. So it is with worship; we cannot offer true worship without love, and our passion for the Lord is magnified in our worship.

To express genuine love through prayer, we must be sold out to following the Lord by walking in His ways and living with the consciousness that we live to please the One who has captivated our hearts. We must make conscious decisions about nurturing our love for Him; this can only happen if we submit ourselves to living by His Word. When it is time to express ourselves through worship, our worship will be authentic. He deserves all of who we are and not some of us. I love Him wholeheartedly!

Destructive Love:

It Will Destroy You if You Let It

"How long will you people turn my glory into shame? How long will you love delusions and seek false gods." (Psalm 4:2 – NIV).

Love can become destructive and very damaging if channeled in the wrong way. I call it "unhealthy love." This kind of love is when we love the things of the world more than the things of God, or we love to please man more than pleasing God. Esteeming our personal needs and ambitions in a place higher than God and the advancement of His Kingdom is idolatry. Love that dissuades you from loving the Lord, as the scriptures explain, is destructive, unhealthy, and can ultimately destroy your life.

It is impossible to say we love God with our whole heart and love vain things simultaneously. Whom and what you love is whom and what you will give your devotion and loyalty to. We cannot be divided in our dedication and expect to offer worship that is acceptable to God. Our Father deserves honor and glory that pleases Him. When we love our riches and wealth more than God, it becomes an abomination to the Lord. Let Jesus be the object of our gaze!

Your Love Is My Canopy:

True Love Covers

"The LORD watches over all who love him, but all the wicked he will destroy." (Psalm 145:20 – NIV).

"Moses built an altar and called it The LORD is my Banner." (Exodus 17:15 – NIV).

The love of the Lord covers and overshadows His children because He loves us with an everlasting love. The love of the Lord is a safe place; a hiding place during a storm; an assurance that all is well through trials and tribulations. His love is perfect; so perfect that it casts out any fear of our past, fear of today, and fear of the future. Fear is a spirit; it can intimidate you, preventing you from making progress.

We are preserved by the love of God, and He spreads His love as a banner and canopy over the righteous. He covers us with His love and protects us from harm and danger. He loves and defends us. We can grow in our love for the Lord and show it by standing up for the gospel of Jesus Christ through our lifestyle, speech, and actions. When you are confused and threatened by the enemy, the Lord will cover you, and everything will align according to His will.

MY REFLECTIONS

MY DECISIONS

"I will instruct you and teach you in the way you should go, I will counsel you with my loving eye on you." (Psalm 32:8 – NIV).

Section Seven

Joy

Joyful Laughter:

It Is Real

"He will yet fill your mouth with laughter and your lips with shouts of joy." (Job 8:21 – NIV).

In Christ, there is unspeakable joy and healing. Oh, how the Father fills our days and lives with unforgettable moments filled with laughter and lasting memories. Have you ever experienced laughter in the Holy Ghost? It feels like angels tickling you, and you have this contagious, uncontrollable laughter. Unfortunately, it is hard to find genuine joy in this generation. People want a quick fix; they want to feel happy for a season, but joy is long-lasting, and it brightens up the day of anyone who encounters you. Only God can bring us genuine laughter and joy that can surpass the pressures and mishaps this world offers.

True joy and laughter are not within our riches and wealth; they cannot be found in our accolades, connections, or social status but in Christ. To communicate joy in worship, we must first learn to always be joyful in all situations and remember that His joy makes us strong.

Joy is one of the fruit of the Spirit, and He is ever ready to produce that fruit in us, if we are willing to cultivate it. So, trust in the Lord to fill your heart!

Fullness of Joy:

It is Unstoppable

"You make known to me the path of life; you will fill me with joy in your presence, with eternal pleasures at your right hand." (Psalm 16:11- NIV).

Happiness is temporary, but the fullness of joy can be found only in the presence of the Lord. Everything we need or will ever need is found there. For our joy to be complete, we must become familiar with and desire the presence of the Lord. The Holy Spirit must become our friend and trustworthy associate. This is so important as a worshiper or a worship leader; we must learn how to cultivate the presence of God. It will cost you time, effort, obedience, and, other times, sacrifice.

Sometimes, the Holy Spirit will demand more of your time, and we must obey. Consider these times to be precious moments with your Father. Fellowshipping with Abba Father is more beneficial than passing the time on unprofitable things. We experience the fullness of joy in His presence and become more like Him. Today, make up your mind to ask the Holy Spirit to lead you into God's presence. In His company, our joy is complete, and we have life-changing experiences.

Joy of Salvation:

I Found Joy When I Found Jesus

"Restore to me the joy of your salvation and grant me a willing spirit, to sustain me." (Psalm 51:12 – NIV).

When we become new believers by receiving the Lord Jesus Christ as our Lord and Savior, we experience such great joy in our hearts. The world is unknown; the sky is more transparent, stars shine brighter, and our spirits soar. We get excited about our new birth, and our adoption into the Kingdom of God is fantastic, but somewhere along our journey as Christians, we lose that vigor and joy we once had. Like the Psalmist, we make a mistake by sinning and no longer feel that joy in our hearts, and we fall into self-condemnation. Other times, our focus shifts, and we begin to doubt the very existence of God. We must realize that we need God's help. We need to depend on Him to maintain the joy of salvation.

The Lord will tug on our hearts to change our ways when we face challenges, death, sicknesses, and mishaps, and lose faith—church and Christianity becoming bywords. Today, if you find yourself in that category, God wants to restore that joy you once had. He is a God of second chances.

Tears:

Sometimes a Good Thing

"Those who sow with tears will reap with songs of joy." (Psalm 126:5 – NIV).

Tears are shed during a difficult time; when you are facing challenging circumstances, or when you are going through a painful situation. We cannot control what happens in life's journey, but we can control how we respond to any negative situation or event that brings us to tears. It could be sorrow, hurt, the death of a loved one, disappointment, heartbreak, or tragedy. What causes you to cry should not last forever. It is written in Ecclesiastes 3:1, "There is a time for everything, and a season for every activity under the heavens" (NIV). Being joyful is part of the package of salvation, and there is joy after any unhappy situation.

If you must cry, go ahead; if you must mourn, go ahead. One thing you can be sure of is that joy is coming as a harvest. We also cry when we are happy, excited, grateful, and satisfied, and God turns our tears of pain into tears of joy. Tears are not always unnecessary; God sees our tears when we cry, and it moves His heart. Tears will bring you relief and free your heart. Remember to put your head on His shoulder and allow Him to heal you in the name of Jesus.

Joy Beyond the Trials:

This Won't Last Forever

"Consider it pure joy, my brothers and sisters, whenever you face trials of many kinds." (James 1:2 – NIV).

When we take our eyes off the problem and look beyond the suffering and trials, we can see the greater purpose of the Lord. If we allow Him to finish His work in us, after the process, we will see massive growth in our lives, and we will be more robust and mature. Trials, temptations, and tribulations can be used to build up character in a worshipper's life; during these times, we learn patience. We know how to persevere, though we suffer long during these seasons. It may be painful, but we must remember that God is making us into something more beautiful on the inside. It may not seem like it, but we must consciously look to Jesus and keep our eyes on the prize ahead. When our mindset changes about troubles, and we embrace them as part of life, we can browse through the process. Only then will the joy of the Lord well up in us like a fountain that many can drink from.

MY REFLECTIONS

MY DECISIONS

_____
_____
_____
_____
_____
_____
_____
_____
_____
_____
_____
_____
_____
_____
_____
_____
_____
_____
_____
_____
_____
_____
_____

"I will instruct you and teach you in the way you should go, I will counsel you with my loving eye on you." (Psalm 32:8 – NIV).

Section Eight

The Presence of God

Lifeless Without You:

I Come Alive in Your Presence

"Do not cast me from your presence or take your Holy Spirit from me." (Psalm 51:11 – NIV).

Life has no meaning without the presence of the Holy Spirit. A worshipper without an intimate relationship with the Father is like a walking dead. The presence of God is our lifeline, and we must develop a routine that helps us build a relationship with Him and maintain that relationship as we grow spiritually. We sometimes err by walking in disobedience to the Word of God. We must repent immediately, realize we are wrong, and seek His presence.

The presence of the Lord gives us such completeness, spiritual satisfaction, healing, and peace that this world cannot provide. It permeates your entire being and makes you whole. Our goal as worshippers is to lead God's people into His presence, and we can only lead someone to a place that we have been before. If a worshiper does not know the presence of God, they cannot teach someone about His existence. We must also learn to run to God instead of running away from the presence of God. It is in His company that we can also find help and forgiveness. When you fall, ask the Holy Spirit to help you rise.

His Presence:

God With Us

"Then Moses said to him, "If your Presence does not go with us, do not send us up from here." (Exodus 33:15 – NIV).

When the children of Israel turned away from God and made a golden calf to worship, they separated themselves from the presence of God. Moses pleaded and interceded on their behalf, and God agreed to accompany them to the promised land. Like the children of Israel, we sometimes separate ourselves from the presence of God by our actions, and we ignore the very existence of God, our Father. The presence of God is His Holy Spirit who walks with us. Being separated from Him means we have no sense of direction or guidance. He knows the future and is the only one who can reveal Jesus to us. Without a revelation of who Jesus is and the price He paid for us on the cross of calvary, our worship is meaningless. We need Him every second of our lives.

The presence of God is not there for occasions, worship events, and services; He is here to keep us connected to the Father. If we want to be used of God in worship, we must put aside idols and worship Him alone. Keep seeking Him and loving His presence!

Entrance:

Gladness is the Entrance Way

"Worship the LORD with gladness; come before him with joyful songs." (Psalm 100:2 – NIV).

We have a great privilege to enter the presence of the Lord. The Word of God has made known to us the way God wants us to join His presence. Entering the presence of God must be done with gladness of heart; this means it will be challenging to enter His company without bliss. When pain and sorrow fill your heart, come to Him, remembering that He knows everything will work out for your good. This demands a change of thought, and faith must be expressed by daring life's challenges and consciously deciding to be joyful and entering His presence. This is not to downplay a challenging time of transition, but I would like to remind you that God's presence is a place where you can find all you need to make this process bearable.

Enter His presence, knowing that He is fully aware of you and what you are going through. It is easy to be glad when all is well and things are working out the way you want them; the testimonies and breakthroughs help, and we can glide in without stress. Remember that the God of the breakthrough is also the same God who sees you in your struggle. Enter In!

No Hiding Place:

But I Desire to Hide Sometimes

"Where can I go from your Spirit? Where can I flee from your presence?" (Psalm 139:7 – NIV).

Abba Father is omnipresent, which means He is present everywhere. There is no unreachable place in this world or outside of this world. Darkness is like light before Him. When we feel alone, remember that He sees you. He is right there with you. When you feel like an outcast, misfit or feel like people don't accept you, He is right there with you. When guilt settles in, we may be tempted to look for a place to hide from the presence of God, like Adam and Eve. You should ask yourself, *"Why would I want to run away from the presence of God?"* Consciously, you may not think of a reason for running from the presence of God, but sin causes us to run from Him through our actions after we make a mistake. We draw away from the things of God, believing the devil's lies that God does not love us anymore. Just remember that you can't run or hide from Him; He loves you no matter what you have done; therefore, run to Him and not from Him.

Glory Belongs to God:

Following His Ways Brings Him Glory

"so that no one may boast before him." (1 Corinthians 1:29 – NIV).

God has orchestrated things in such an excellent way that creation declares His glory. He chooses people that the world considers the "nobodies," the rejected ones; I call them the "Peters of our time." He uses ordinary men to communicate to the world that He does exist.

The calling of God is without favoritism. He does not pour out to a specific group of people from a particular country because He prefers them over others. God calls all men regardless of cultural differences, ethnicity, geographical location, or race. He calls those who will answer the call and avail themselves to pursue their purpose. Worshipers are in a unique office; we artistically create a path for others to enter God's presence. This is not a calling that is better than others but a privilege and immense responsibility. We are to take the call seriously and do our work diligently. Keep in mind that we are just stewards, and in all that we do, the platforms we stand on, be it great or small, we must point people to our Father because the glory belongs to Him.

MY REFLECTIONS

MY DECISIONS

"I will instruct you and teach you in the way you should go, I will counsel you with my loving eye on you." (Psalm 32:8 – NIV).

Section Nine

Chosen

He Chose Me:

Born For This Purpose

"But you are a chosen people, a royal priesthood, a holy nation, God's special possession, that you may declare the praises of him who called you out of darkness into his wonderful light." (1 Peter 2:9 – NIV).

We must embrace the truth that God, in His infinite wisdom, chose us for a special purpose. We believed ourselves to be the ones called to offer the worship He desires. Though He could have chosen animals, He selected us instead. We are royalty. He gave us a high calling and made us holy by the blood of Jesus. He went further and made us special to tell of the good things He has done for us. We are to tell the world of the goodness of God. We are His people, tasked with making His works known to the world. Our messages should be deliberate with gratitude, telling the world how He saved and called us from a place of damnation to a new life in Him.

Our gratitude must translate into the things we do; we must tell our story of salvation to the world by recounting the goodness of God through our songs. Abba Father did what only He could do. He had a plan before we were in existence.

No Other Opinion:

Chosen to Bear Fruit

"You did not choose me, but I chose you and appointed you so that you might go and bear fruit—fruit that will last—and so that whatever you ask in my name the Father will give you." (John 15:16 – NIV).

When God decided to choose you, He did not need the opinion of anyone. He chose and placed you where He knew it was the best soil for you to bear fruit. He knew where you needed to be held and how He would use you. Sometimes, we think that if we were born in the western world, the chances of impacting our world would be more significant. God is no respecter of persons, and our place of birth and family background does not negate His plans for our lives. The most important thing is to keep in mind that God chose, called, and strategically positioned you in the body of Christ to make an impact. Our skin color, place of birth, geographic location, and accent do not change His mind about us. When we bear fruit, it opens the door to answering prayers. Everything we do must reflect the reason why we were saved. Know your identity!

Spoken For:

I Am His

"For you are a people holy to the LORD your God. The LORD your God has chosen you out of all the peoples on the face of the earth to be his people, his treasured possession." (Deuteronomy 7:6 – NIV).

We are part of the family of God. God chose us in all our frailty. Remember, what matters is what God says about you. You are unique; you are made in His image and likeness. You house the Spirit of God; you are the temple of God's presence. God is not one who lacks wisdom, so He meant everything He did. He is serious about the calling on your life, and how He wants you to impact this generation. He has recorded all the days of your life, and it is no mistake that you are a minister, worship leader, or worker in the house of God. Embrace who you are and walk in it. Don't let anything or anyone intimidate you and talk you out of your calling. The God of the universe has called you by name and put His Spirit in you. The kingdom of darkness, your parents or associates did not have to recommend you. He did it all by Himself!

Before My Parents:

I Am His Treasured Possession

> *"For you are a people holy to the LORD your God. Out of all the peoples on the face of the earth, the LORD has chosen you to be his treasured possession." (Deuteronomy 14:2 – NIV).*

It is such an honor to have the assurance that the God of the universe—the Creator of the heavens and the earth—would choose a group of people and call them His prized possession. He did this for the children of Israel, and today, all who believe in Him are a part of that selection. Think about it for a minute; you did not have to beg your way through, negotiate, or pay money to be a part of this great, big family. He chose you and me because He loves us.

Before my father met my mother, God had me in mind and had a plan for me. He used my parents as vessels to bring me into this world, just as He used Mary, the mother of Jesus. If God can choose us to be His cherished people on earth, we ought to bless and worship Him in Spirit and truth; it's the best we can do. We owe Him that much!

Before the Earth's Foundation:

He Was Intentional

"For he chose us in him before the creation of the world to be holy and blameless in his sight. In love." (Ephesians 1:4-5 –NIV).

Even before there was a speckle of you, Abba Father, in His infinite wisdom, loved you with an everlasting love. This scripture shows that before God created the world, He loved and chose us. This is so profound, knowing that while He made the land, seas, and animals, His love was placed upon us. We are loved and chosen to walk in the holiness of God.

The Lord Jesus was our means of entry, and He remains our way of staying. Without Him, we can never be a part of this. God did not need our opinion; sometimes, we think we are not good enough for some things and some positions in life. Rejoice today that your election did not depend on how you feel and what you think about yourself. Regardless of your outlook on life, remember that you are unique.

MY REFLECTIONS

MY DECISIONS

"I will instruct you and teach you in the way you should go, I will counsel you with my loving eye on you." (Psalm 32:8 – NIV).

Section Ten

Total Surender

Self-Denial:

It's Not About Me

Then Jesus said to his disciples, "Whoever wants to be my disciple must deny themselves and take up their cross and follow me." (Matthew 16:24 – NIV).

We have an opportunity to follow Jesus, but we must realize that serving the Lord will require laying down our ambitions and walking in His ways. It requires us to deny ourselves; sometimes, what we deny ourselves can be the most precious things in life or the costliest items. We must keep in mind that if we must walk in the steps of Jesus Christ, imitate His ways, and have His mindset, we must relinquish all that does not align with the Scriptures.

The cross was meant for criminals and lawbreakers. Jesus took the cross on our behalf, and He is calling us to walk in His shoes in the sense that we accept the fact that we may be falsely accused and not try to justify ourselves. He is calling us to walk in a degrading place for His sake and not try to pull our way out. It is part of our worship to let go of our rights for the sake of Jesus Christ. Worship will cost you!

We Are His Workmanship:

He Makes Me Willing by His Spirit

"for it is God who works in you to will and to act in order to fulfill his good purpose." (Philippians 2:13 – NIV).

No man can successfully serve the Lord within the flesh or with carnality. The things of the spirit cannot be controlled or pursued with a carnal mentality. This is important because God gave us His Holy Spirit as a Helper. Every believer must allow themselves to be influenced by the Holy Spirit because He was sent to enable us to do exploits and outstanding works on the face of the earth for the Kingdom of God.

How does God work in us? He makes us willing by the power of His Holy Spirit to bring Him pleasure in many ways, including worship. This means that for the work of God to be manifested in our lives, we must learn how to cultivate a relationship with the Holy Spirit. The Holy Spirit knows what the Father's needs are, and He can reveal the deep things of God to us. He is also present as our Help and He teaches us all things. We must submit to the Holy Spirit; that is the only way to please God.

Doing His Will:

Not Walking Without Direction

"Not everyone who says to me, 'Lord, Lord,' will enter the kingdom of heaven, but only the one who does the will of my Father who is in heaven." (Matthew 7:21 –NIV).

We can get carried away by the flare of ministry and what we see with our naked eyes. We need to be vigilant in these end times, knowing that many have come in the name of the Lord, and many will claim that the Lord calls them to the extent of professing to be the Christ. Scriptures tell us that not everyone who says the name of the Lord or claims to belong to Christ is truly His; we must be discerning to understand.

We need the gift of discernment to know what spirit a person is operating under. We can all testify to the unbiblical portrayals of the Bible and the faithful servants of God on social media. The gospel of Jesus Christ is under attack, and we must be wise. This is the time to work out our salvation with fear and trembling. Be like the sons of Issachar, searching the Scriptures and holding on to what is good. As Worshippers, we must stick with sound doctrine!

Dangerous Game:

Lose It for the Sake of Christ

"For whoever wants to save their life will lose it, but whoever loses their life for me will find it." (Matthew 16:25 – NIV).

The Gospel of Jesus Christ is profitable, and many have taken advantage of this opportunity. When we are called to the ministry, we serve God's people. Service will cost you much, but the Father gives you the grace and strength to accomplish what He has assigned you to. We must not abuse this privilege we are given. We must serve God with all our hearts, soul, and strength. We can never take someone before the throne of grace by our worship if we are not dedicated to the Lord. We must lose what we call life. There should be nothing more precious than Elohim- God the Father, God the Son, and God the Holy Spirit.

Choosing to do the will of God may cost you friends, relatives, loved ones, associates, colleagues, and things you cherish the most, but it is more dangerous to hold on than to let go. When you surrender to Christ, you can experience life's fullness and all it offers. When you hold on, you lose everything. Total surrender is required!

Surrendering is in Our Doing:

Walking in His Ways

"Do not merely listen to the word, and so deceive yourselves. Do what it says." (James 1:22 – NIV).

Surrendering to the Lord is an expression of our love for Him. He said, *"If you love me, keep my commands." (John 14:15 – NIV).* The act of surrendering is total abandonment and submission to the authority of Christ. We let go of our rights and our ability to fight and allow the Spirit of God to lead us as the Father gives direction. When we surrender to Christ, it must show in all we do. Our actions are essential. We cannot say we have surrendered and still maintain our old ways of doing things.

Some principles we learned in the world cannot be applied in the Kingdom of God. We must, therefore, learn the ways of our Master by obeying His instructions. We must use the Scriptures in our lives by living how Christ wants us to live. This is why we cannot sing worldly music in a church and expect a spiritual response. It is not possible because we have now switched sides. Let's surrender all to the Lord, including our ambition of becoming worldly musicians, doing ungodly things, and desecrating the altar of worship.

MY REFLECTIONS

MY DECISIONS

_____
_____
_____
_____
_____
_____
_____
_____
_____
_____
_____
_____
_____
_____
_____
_____
_____
_____
_____
_____
_____
_____

"I will instruct you and teach you in the way you should go, I will counsel you with my loving eye on you." (Psalm 32:8 – NIV).

Section Eleven

Seek Him First

First Things First:

We Must Keep This in Mind

"But seek first his kingdom and his righteousness, and all these things will be given to you as well." (Matthew 6:33 – NIV).

To seek means to diligently pursue and exert every effort to obtain what we are after, which is the Kingdom of God and His righteousness above all else. Our priorities must be set straight by putting the Kingdom of God first in all we do. God knows the motives of every man, and He examines our hearts. He knows when we approach Him for just the blessings He provides, and when we are chasing after Him. Let us change our mindset about approaching the throne of grace and why we approach His throne.

When we focus on the things of God, nothing can be withheld from us. We must have the right attitude and godly character when we strive after the things of God. Then we will experience God and enjoy the benefits of being a child of the highest God. Most of the time, we approach God, our Father, when we want something, especially when we are in trouble, but we must unlearn the ways of manipulation to get what we want and become genuine seekers of the Kingdom of God.

My Daily Bread:

All Day, A Part of Me

"Look to the LORD and his strength; seek his face always." (1 Chronicles 16:11 – NIV).

We are not born with an attitude to seek the face of God daily. The journey begins when we are reconciled with our Maker. This is a lifelong, daily quest to know the Lord better. We learn His ways by studying the Scriptures. The Word of God reveals who our Father is, and we understand how He loves us and what He has made available to us. Getting to know the Lord will shape our relationship with Him, and we get to know His ways, which provoke change in our lives.

We must learn to cultivate the spiritual routine of communing with our Father. A believer who seeks God is a person who is developing a life of prayer. Prayer is our way of communicating with the Father; this is an essential part of our journey in seeking Him. Besides learning the Scriptures, we must learn to pray the Scriptures, keeping in mind that scriptural prayers rule the spirit world and grant you access to the throne of grace. We talk to our Father, and we dominate the heavens by Scriptures.

It's a Heart Thing:

He Knows My Thoughts

"Then you will call on me and come and pray to me, and I will listen to you." (Jeremiah 29:12-13 – NIV).

When we worship, we call on the Lord's name. In everything we do, we call on His name, for there is no other name we can call on. The issue is not when or how loud we get when we call, how often we call, or how knowledgeable we are. It is how we call upon Him. We can call on Him and seek His face a million times, but if our hearts are not aligned with what we say or do, we are just wasting our time. Our hearts must be in everything we do as believers.

When a believer's heart is filled with the Scriptures, and our motives are pure, there will be nothing we cannot receive from our heavenly Father. The way to finding God and seeking His Kingdom is with sincerity of heart, having an honest desire to get to know Him. It is only when we see a person that we know what He likes.

Seeking Him or Other Things:

Is He First?

"The LORD looks down from heaven on all mankind to see if there are any who understand, any who seek God." (Psalm 14:2 – NIV).

The Lord is interested in His children seeking Him. He takes His time to search out genuine seekers and true worshipers. If we desire to seek the face of our heavenly Father, we must begin by searching the Scriptures. Studying the Word of God helps us to get to know our Father and learn what is expected of us as His chosen ones. Understanding will pave the way and make it easy to walk in the will of God. God wants His children to seek Him. He is equally concerned about our needs, and we can all testify of His goodness in our lives as we serve Him faithfully.

Can God see us seeking His face or seeking His blessings? When we seek God, the things we need will be freely ours. Most of us misunderstand prayer requests when seeking Abba Father. When we present a prayer request to God, we ask Him to fulfill a need, but seeking God is seeking a time of fellowship and worship without presenting a petition. Let us not become seekers of things but become seekers of God. He loves it when we seek Him!

My Heart's Desire:

To Seek Him

"One thing I ask from the LORD, this only do I seek: that I may dwell in the house of the LORD all the days of my life, to gaze on the beauty of the LORD and to seek him in his temple." (Psalm 27:4 – NIV).

Seeking God comes from an earnest desire to know and fellowship with Him. We are familiar with asking God for a blessing, breakthrough, miracle, or intervention to benefit our families and us. We get anxious and are willing to do anything to get what we want from God when we need something. Sometimes, I wonder what a more significant benefit it would be if we asked God to give us spiritual things and not earthly things that are perishable.

David, the Psalmist, prayed for one thing: to dwell in God's presence and seek His guidance all the days of his life. As we seek God for earthly blessings, let us also deeply pursue intimacy with God and the spiritual nourishment that keeps us anchored; this becomes our soul's steadfast anchor. Every believer should nurture a fervent desire to stay firmly rooted in Christ. Not forsaking the assembling of the saints, engaging in our church's spiritual activities and services not only brings stability to our lives but ensures that we remain fruitful for the Kingdom of God, even into our later years.

MY REFLECTIONS

MY DECISIONS

"I will instruct you and teach you in the way you should go, I will counsel you with my loving eye on you." (Psalm 32:8 – NIV).

Section 12

A New Song

A Song of Transformation:

Telling My Life Story

"He put a new song in my mouth, a hymn of praise to our God. Many will see and fear the LORD and put their trust in him." (Psalm 40:3 –NIV).

Who can deliver us from the grips of hell and the tumults of life? The Psalmist began to sing a new song that showed God's deliverance in his life. He counted the things that the Lord had done in his life. This song reflects God's mercy and mighty works in the life of a believer. This reveals that the Lord's deeds can fill your heart with joy and inspire you to sing beautiful melodies about His goodness and mercy.

This is what we do; we tell of the goodness of God in songs, hymns, and spiritual songs. When you go through a challenge or face a situation that is supposed to alter your life, when God steps in and pulls you out, you ought to tell the world about it. Our victories and testimonies are to be heard. We are to tell our stories of how God delivered us, and someone might be saved. So, sing! Sing of the goodness of God! Tell of His might in your song!

With My Soul:

With My Spirit

And Mary said: "My soul glorifies the Lord." (Luke 1:46-47 – NIV).

A man's soul is composed of his mind, emotions, and intellect. A man's soul is the place of interaction with the world. We express ourselves with our feelings. We have been given this incredible ability to show what we mean, and God loves it when we offer true worship with true emotions. Keep in mind that being emotional is an intimate part of worship.

Since worship is an expression of love, the feelings we express during worship come from the heart. Genuine emotions erupt from the heart and not just from our souls. The heart and soul must be aligned in worship. If the soul is the seat of our intellect, then we must worship with the understanding of who God is.

Knowledge is power, and it makes our worship effective. We cannot worship without understanding God. A worshiper must know who God is to lead God's people to that place of intimacy with Him in worship. We cannot sing about a great God if we do not understand the greatness of God. Knowledge will enhance your worship, so get it!

Sing of His Greatness:

The World is Waiting

"Sing to the LORD a new song; sing to the LORD, all the earth. Sing to the LORD, praise his name; proclaim his salvation day after day. Declare his glory among the nations, his marvelous deeds among all peoples." (Psalm 96:1-3 – NIV).

When we sing, our songs must tell of the greatness of God. Music is a great communication tool. Politicians, hospitals, social media influencers, and many other institutions use it. As worshippers, we are given an incredible gift of music. The content and lyrics of our songs must point people to Christ and Christ alone. He is the reason why we sing. Our melodies are catalysts to creating an awareness of God, our Father, declaring His greatness on earth.

We are to promote the Gospel of Jesus Christ with our songs. Our testimonies are so powerful that when shared with the world, they give understanding and encourage others. Let us not be ashamed to share the goodness of God with the world. Singing a new song means we will have new things occurring in our lives that we can sing about. They may not always be pleasant, but our trust in God brings us out. Sing a new song regardless.

He Has Done Marvelous Things:

My Heart Sing

"A psalm. Sing to the LORD a new song, for he has done marvelous things; his right hand and his holy arm have worked salvation for him." (Psalm 98:1 – NIV).

We serve an amazing God; His works, creativity, and faithfulness speak for themselves. The verse above encourages us to sing a new song because of the things the Lord does. He is a loving Father and a God who has never lost a battle. He takes pleasure in being victorious and giving us victory over the enemy. He is a God who takes down the pharaohs of the world; He conquers the enemy and causes kings of the earth to marvel. Even before time, no one or nothing has been able to stand up to our God. Let us sing songs about how God has defeated the enemy and the victory we have experienced because of the deliverance of the Lord.

He fights on behalf of His children. He is "a Man of war" (see Exodus 15:3). The psalmist speaks of God's right hand as "the right hand that does mighty things." (see Psalm 118:16). His writing is mighty, and when He uses His hands to fight, we can only expect victory. Sing of His victory!

Making Melodies:

The Sound of Instruments

"I will sing a new song to you, my God; on the ten-stringed lyre I will make music to you." (Psalm 144:9 – NIV).

The Bible is clear on how we are to sing about and worship God. We can discover ways and instructions in the Word of God regarding music. We learned in our readings that God desires us to sing of many things, including His greatness. The Scriptures show us how God wants us to sing to Him. He is a God of melody; He loves beautiful music. If it were not so, there would not always be worship in heaven. The angels, the twenty-four elders, and living creatures worship God continually, singing beautiful songs unto the Lord, and yet, God wants us to join in the worship with our voices and instruments.

I believe that in heaven, there is no mistake, no time for rehearsals, and no mistake in singing another note other than what should be sung. God wants us to sing in all our musical mistakes. He wants to hear you sing with instrumentation. If the Scriptures command us to make music and sing, then the capacity is already in us, and the Holy Spirit will help us develop our gifts.

MY REFLECTIONS

MY DECISIONS

"I will instruct you and teach you in the way you should go, I will counsel you with my loving eye on you." (Psalm 32:8 – NIV).

Conclusion

It is evident that worship leaders and ministers of the gospels are not immune to painful experiences and adverse situations, but God has provided a pathway to recovery and growth. He wants you whole as you minister through songs and the word.

When you are going through a season of hurt or a difficult time, remember that you must keep your heart pure and guarded from the things that will take the place of pure worship.

In His Presence,
Elenora Mouphouet

About the Author

Pastor Elenora is a multifaceted leader who founded PEMM (Pastor Elenora Mouphouet Ministries), Woman Arise Int'l and serves as the senior pastor of Global Revival Missions, Maryland. Additionally, she is the co-founder and president of Judah's Generation, a worship ministry focused on restoring biblical worship principles and manages City Watch, an online intercessory platform where she leads praying for cities and nations.

Pastor Elenora answered the call to ministry in her youth and has served as a music minister, worship leader, and Christian counselor across various countries. Known for her charismatic approach, she passionately ministers the Word of God, emphasizing prayer, the Word of God, and true worship for life transformation. Her journey in worship is documented in her book, "Free to Worship Liberated to Praise." She is married to Apostle Edward Mouphouet. They reside in the United States of America and are united in their commitment to fulfilling their purposes and advancing the kingdom of God.

www.ingramcontent.com/pod-product-compliance
Lightning Source LLC
Chambersburg PA
CBHW070508090426
42735CB00012B/2699